*Author:*

**Ian Graham** earned a degree in applied physics at City University, London. He then earned a graduate degree in journalism. Since becoming a freelance author and journalist, he has written more than 250 children's nonfiction books.

*Series creator:*

**David Salariya** was born in Dundee, Scotland. He has illustrated a wide range of books and has created and designed many new series for publishers in the UK and overseas. David established The Salariya Book Company in 1989. He lives in Brighton, England, with his wife, illustrator Shirley Willis, and their son, Jonathan.

*Artists:*

Paco Sordo
Bryan Beach

*Editor:*

Jacqueline Ford

© The Salariya Book Company Ltd MMXVIII
No part of this publication may be reproduced in whole or in part, or stored in a retrieval system, or transmitted in any form or by any means, electronic, mechanical, photocopying, recording, or otherwise, without written permission of the publisher. For information regarding permission, write to the copyright holder.

Published in Great Britain in 2018 by
**The Salariya Book Company Ltd**
25 Marlborough Place, Brighton BN1 1UB

ISBN-13: 978-0-531-25833-0 (lib. bdg.) 978-0-531-26903-9 (pbk.)

All rights reserved.
Published in 2018 in the United States
by Franklin Watts
An imprint of Scholastic Inc.

A CIP catalog record for this book is available
from the Library of Congress.

Printed and bound in China.
Printed on paper from sustainable sources.
1 2 3 4 5 6 7 8 9 10 R 27 26 25 24 23 22 21 20 19 18

SCHOLASTIC, FRANKLIN WATTS, and associated logos are trademarks and/or registered trademarks of Scholastic Inc.

PAPER FROM
SUSTAINABLE
FORESTS

# The Science of Prehistoric Giants

## Dinosaurs That Used Size and Armor for Defense

Written by
Ian Graham

Illustrated by
Paco Sordo

Franklin Watts®
An Imprint of Scholastic Inc.

# Contents

| | |
|---|---|
| Introduction | 5 |
| Key Features | 6 |
| Giant Bodies | 8 |
| Jawbreaking Armor | 10 |
| Terrible Tails | 12 |
| Beaks and Teeth | 14 |
| Horrible Horns | 16 |
| Safety in Numbers | 18 |
| Tiny Brains | 20 |
| Dino Senses | 22 |
| Sounding Off | 24 |
| Coloring In | 26 |
| Finding Fossils | 28 |
| Glossary | 30 |
| Index | 32 |

Stegosaurus

| Triassic: 252–201 mya | Jurassic: 201–145 mya |

*Mya = Million years ago*

# Introduction

Dinosaurs ruled the earth for millions of years. They appeared more than 240 million years ago and reigned supreme for more than 170 million years. Compared to that, our species, *homo sapiens*, has existed for only 200,000 years—a speck in time compared to the dinosaurs.

The Age of Dinosaurs began during a time in Earth's early history called the Triassic Period and continued through the Jurassic and Cretaceous Periods. These amazing creatures died out at the end of the Cretaceous Period, about 65 million years ago.

The first dinosaurs were small meat eaters, or carnivores, that snapped up bugs and other small creatures. Then some dinosaurs started eating plants. They were herbivores. Over millions of years, bigger and bigger dinosaurs evolved. The plant eaters, or herbivores, were the biggest by far. Some of them were awesome giants more than 100 feet (30 meters) long, and standing taller than a house. They were the biggest creatures that have ever lived on land.

Triceratops

Cretaceous: 145-65 mya

## Standing Upright

Dinosaurs stood on top of straight legs. Legs like this could carry a lot of weight, making it possible for truly gigantic dinosaurs to evolve. Their legs held their body above the ground and let them walk more easily compared to more primitive creatures like lizards and crocodiles.

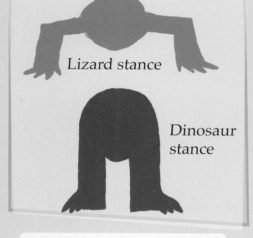

Lizard stance

Dinosaur stance

The dinosaurs competed for food and territory with a variety of other land animals, including lizards, crocodiles, flying reptiles, mammals, and even swarms of giant insects.

# Key Features

The giant plant-eating dinosaurs had a special set of features that made them some of the most successful creatures of their world. Their crushing weight was supported by massive pillar-like leg bones. Broad foot pads spread the animal's weight on the ground. Specialized teeth were shaped for gathering vegetation, and a huge gut was ideal for digesting tough plants. The immense size of these huge creatures meant that they could bulldoze their way wherever they wanted to go in search of food, and few creatures were powerful enough to stop them.

# Walking on Four Legs

The first dinosaurs were bipedal—they walked on two legs. They used their muscular tail like a third leg to help them balance. As the plant-eating dinosaurs evolved into bigger and bigger creatures, they walked on four legs to support their immense weight—they were quadrupedal.

It takes guts to be a dinosaur!

## Titanic Gut

The big plant-eating dinosaurs had a huge belly for holding lots of the vegetation that they ate. Countless trillions of microscopic bacteria in their gut broke down the plants to let the nutrients out. So, the biggest dinosaurs relied on the smallest living organisms to break down their food.

## Survival Tactics

Giant plant-eating dinosaurs were too big to hide from predators, but they may have used their immense size and weight to their advantage. Any predator that came too close risked being trampled underfoot.

Go away or I'll flatten you.

There is a limit to how big a land animal can grow before its bones and muscles can't support its weight anymore. The biggest dinosaurs may have approached this limit.

# Giant Bodies

The biggest dinosaurs were gigantic plant-eating creatures called sauropods, and the biggest sauropods were titanosaurs. Some titanosaurs were more than 100 feet (30 m) long and stood as high as a seven-story building. They may have weighed up to 100 tons (90 metric tons), or maybe even more. They had a long snakelike neck with a small head on the end. The titanosaurs appeared near the end of the Age of Dinosaurs and quickly spread all over the world. Many of the biggest titanosaur remains are found in South America.

## The Biggest Dinosaur?

The biggest dinosaur found so far was discovered in Argentina in 2014. It was a titanosaur that died about 100 million years ago. It was 130 feet (40 m) long and weighed 84 tons (76 MT). It was not fully grown, so there must have been even bigger titanosaurs!

## Cold or Warm Blood?

We used to think that dinosaurs were cold-blooded. They basked in the sun to warm their body. Then scientists found clues that dinosaurs might have been warm-blooded, heated by warmth from within their own body. More evidence is needed before we'll really know the truth.

I'm a warmer-saurus.

I'm a well-balanced guy.

## Long Necks and Tails

The giant plant-eating dinosaurs held their head out in front of them at the end of a long neck. Swinging their neck from side to side let them reach lots of vegetation while saving energy by standing in one place. Their equally long tail balanced the weight of their neck.

About 1,000 species of extinct dinosaurs have been found, but scientists think there may be hundreds more that are yet to be discovered.

## Famous Fossil Finds

The first remains of a giant sauropod called Argentinosaurus were found in 1987 in the north of Patagonia, in Argentina. The rancher who found it thought he'd stumbled across a huge piece of ancient wood.

The word dinosaur was invented in 1842 by a British scientist, Richard Owen, who realized that these beings were extinct creatures and not giant people or dragons, as some people had previously thought.

## Ampelosaurus

Many of the biggest dinosaurs were covered with a suit of armor made of bone. One of them was a creature called Ampelosaurus. It had bony lumps, spikes, and plates all over its body. Armored skin protected the big, slow plant eaters against bites and slashes from sharp teeth and claws.

# Jawbreaking Armor

The big plant-eating dinosaurs couldn't move as fast as the predators that hunted them. And they didn't have a predator's flesh-tearing teeth or claws to fight off an attack. They had to protect themselves in other ways. Some dinosaurs developed thick armored skin. The armor came in all shapes and sizes. There were overlapping scales, flat plates, long spikes, and knobby lumps. These bony pieces of skin are called osteoderms. You can see osteoderm armor today if you look at a crocodile or alligator.

# Stegosaur

Stegosaurs were plant-eating dinosaurs with rows of bony plates along their backs. Scientists are still trying to figure out what these plates were for. They were too soft to be armor. They might have controlled the dinosaur's temperature, like radiators, or they might have helped stegosaurs to see each other.

*Don't get my back up!*

# Ankylosaur

Ankylosaurs and their close relatives, nodosaurs, were a group of armored plant-eating dinosaurs. They were built like tanks. Their broad, low-slung body, head, and tail were covered with bony lumps, plates, and spikes. Any attacker foolish enough to bite an ankylosaur or nodosaur risked breaking its teeth.

# Fascinating Fact

A dinosaur called Euoplocephalus was so completely armored that it even had armored eyelids! The only way to kill it was to flip it onto its back and attack its soft belly.

*I don't roll over for anyone!*

A dinosaur's name describes what the creature was like. The dinosaur with the longest name is Micropachycephalosaurus. It means small, thick-headed lizard.

11

# Terrible Tails

## Whip Tails

No one can be sure how dinosaurs behaved because no one has ever seen one alive, but it is possible that the giant plant eaters used their long tail as a whiplike weapon when they were attacked. But some scientists disagree with this, because it would have damaged the tail too much.

**M**any of the big, lumbering plant-eating dinosaurs looked like easy meat for the killers that hunted them. But some of the plant eaters had a secret weapon—their tail. A long tail made a very good whip to knock a predator off its feet. A big, beefy tail was also powerful enough to break an attacker's bones. Some dinosaur tails evolved into even more dangerous weapons with bony spikes or clubs at the end. They could cause severe injuries to any attacker that came too close.

## Club Tails

Some of the big sauropods and armored ankylosaurs had a big ball of bone at the end of their tail. Research on how hard they could swing their tail club shows that they probably couldn't kill a big predator with it, but they could smash its legs.

Stegosaur means "roofed lizard," because scientists used to think that the bony plates on its back lay flat like tiles or shingles on a roof.

## Spiky Tails

Most stegosaurs had a fearsome cluster of sharp, bony spikes at the end of their tail. Scientists know they were used as weapons, because many of them have been found damaged and broken, and killer dinosaur remains have been found with holes made by these spikes.

An ankylosaur's tail club was a massive lump of bone weighing up to 342 pounds (155 kilograms).

## Survival Tactics

When a predator approached a stegosaur, the stegosaur would turn its back to the predator and whip its tail from side to side, to try to stab its tail spikes into the attacker.

13

## On the Menu

When the first dinosaurs appeared, the plants that grew on Earth were very different from today's vegetation. There were no flowering plants or grasses. The dinosaurs fed on ferns, trees called ginkgoes, and primitive plants called horsetails. Later, they fed on conifer trees and palmlike plants called cycads.

# Beaks and Teeth

The plant-eating dinosaurs had specially shaped teeth for eating vegetation. The big sauropod dinosaurs had peg-like teeth for raking leaves from plants. Other plant eaters had birdlike beaks for snipping off vegetation and teeth for chopping it up. Then bacteria in the dinosaur's gut broke down the plants so that they could be digested. Plants are difficult to digest, so dinosaurs had to eat huge amounts of vegetation and keep it inside them for a long time so that bacteria could break it down. That's why some dinosaurs grew to such an enormous size.

The process of using bacteria in the gut to break down plant material is called fermentation.

Leaves for dinner, my favorite!

14

# A Mouthful

An adult human has 32 teeth, but a dinosaur called Triceratops had 800 teeth and duck-billed dinosaurs called hadrosaurs had up to 1,000 teeth! Grinding up vegetation wore down a dinosaur's teeth, so they had to be replaced by new teeth throughout the dinosaur's life.

# Did They Chew?

The sauropod dinosaurs swallowed vegetation without chewing it. Other dinosaurs, including the duck-billed hadrosaurs, chewed vegetation before they swallowed it. As a result, dinosaurs that chewed their food didn't need a huge gut to break it down, and so they didn't grow as big as sauropods.

If you want to be BIG, don't chew!

Duck-billed hadrosaurs had broad grinding teeth to mash plants, while dinosaurs like Triceratops had chopping teeth to cut plants up.

# Can You Believe It?

Some plant-eating dinosaurs swallowed stones known as gastroliths. As the stones tumbled around inside a dinosaur, they may have helped to mash up the plants it had eaten, so that they could be digested more easily.

A Triceratops's horns were made of hard bone in the middle covered with keratin, the same substance that our hair and fingernails are made of.

# Horrible Horns

A group of big plant-eating dinosaurs called ceratopsians had horns on their head. Ceratopsian means "horn face." Scientists think their horns probably evolved to fight rival males and attract mates, but they would probably have been used to fend off attackers, too. There were many ceratopsian species, but the best known and also the biggest was Triceratops. Its name means "three-horned face." Triceratops weighed in at up to 11 tons (10 MT). Its 8-foot-long (2.5 m) head was one of the biggest of any land animal.

## Triceratops

Triceratops was about the size of an elephant, but covered with scaly skin. It had two sharp horns up to 4 feet (1.2 m) long above its eyes and a shorter horn on its nose. Behind its head it had a broad curving plate of bone called a neck frill.

# Other Horned Dinosaurs

Most of the ceratopsian dinosaurs had horns, but the various species looked different from one another. One of them, called Styracosaurus, had one long horn on the end of its nose and a row of horns all around the edge of its bony neck frill.

*If you want to get ahead, get a horn!*

## Can You Believe It?

When the first Triceratops bones were found in 1887, they were mistaken for the remains of a bison. When more bones were found, scientists finally realized that they were from a horned dinosaur.

# When Did They Live?

The first ceratopsian dinosaurs appeared about 160 million years ago during the Jurassic Period. They evolved from one species to another until Triceratops appeared about 70 million years ago. Their horns and armored neck frills must have worked, because they survived until the dinosaurs died out five million years later.

*Get off my land!*

*Quiet, Scaly!*

Triceratops appears to have lived only in the forested river valleys of the western part of North America.

# Safety in Numbers

## How Common Were Herds?

In 1878, the remains of a whole herd of Iguanodons were found in Belgium. One theory is that they fell down a deep ravine and drowned in water at the bottom. Every year there is new evidence of plant-eating dinosaurs traveling in herds, so herding may have been very common.

Many of the big sauropods traveled together in herds. They gathered together to protect themselves and their young, and to look for food and water. We know there were dinosaur herds because sometimes a whole herd died together and the remains of the animals are found together in one place. Another clue comes from dinosaur tracks—footprints left by dinosaurs walking across muddy ground. Lots of footprints all going in the same direction, made at the same time by the same species, show that the animals were traveling together.

*Two's company, three hundred's a herd!*

# Hadrosaur Herds

Thousands of dinosaur footprints were found in Alaska in 2007. They were left behind by hadrosaurs. So many footprints were made at the same time that these hadrosaurs must have been traveling together in a large herd. The herd included animals of all ages and sizes.

# Did Dinosaurs Migrate?

Today, lots of animals go on a long journey every year. It's called migration. There is evidence that some dinosaurs migrated, too. The remains of dinosaurs called Camarasaurus show that they lived on the American plains during the wet season. Then in the dry season they trekked into the mountains.

Plant-eating dinosaurs were safer in herds because some of the dinosaurs could look out for predators while the other members of the herd ate and drank.

# Tiny Brains

Comparing the weight of a creature's brain to the weight of its whole body is a good guide to how intelligent the creature is.

**F**or their immense size, the giant plant-eating dinosaurs had surprisingly small brains. Many of the biggest dinosaurs, like Brachiosaurus, had a brain no bigger than a plum. Some dinosaur brains were as small as a walnut. With such a small brain, even the biggest dinosaurs could not have been very intelligent. The smartest dinosaurs were probably no smarter than a chicken is today. If the dinosaurs hadn't died out, some scientists think they might have had time to develop bigger brains and become smarter, but we will never know.

## Why Were Plant Eaters Not So Smart?

Plants don't run away or fight back, so plant-eating dinosaurs could survive very well with low intelligence. There was no need for them to be very smart. The meat-eating dinosaurs had to outsmart the animals they hunted, so they needed bigger brains and higher intelligence.

Who needs a big brain anyway?

Brain

## Did They Hold Their Heads Up?

Dinosaurs with a long neck might not have been able to lift their head up high. Some scientists think a dinosaur's heart could not possibly have pumped blood with enough force to push it all the way up the dinosaur's neck to its brain, but other scientists disagree.

I've got a head for heights.

A human being is fifty times the weight of its brain, but a big dinosaur might have been 100,000 times the weight of its tiny brain.

## Keeping a Cool Head

When scientists studied well-preserved skulls of dinosaurs such as Stegoceras, they found strangely shaped air passages inside them. These passages didn't seem to have anything to do with the dinosaur's breathing or its sense of smell. Researchers think they carried air to cool the blood and stop the dinosaur's brain from overheating.

## Can You Believe It?

Scientists used to think that the biggest dinosaurs had two brains—one in their head and another in their hips controlling their back legs. Now they know this was wrong. No dinosaur had two brains.

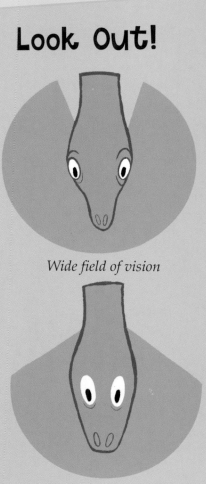

*Wide field of vision*

*Narrow field of vision*

Meat-eating dinosaurs had their eyes close together on the front of their head so that they could focus better on prey in front of them. Plant eaters had their eyes wider apart on the sides of their head. This gave them a better chance of seeing predators approaching, even from behind.

# Dino Senses

Dinosaurs had the same senses as modern animals—sight, smell, hearing, taste, and touch. How well these senses worked depended on which types of dinosaurs were using them. Meat eaters needed better sight, smell, and hearing than the plant eaters they hunted. Compared to meat eaters, the big plant-eating dinosaurs' senses weren't as sharp. Scientists can tell which senses were well-developed and which weren't by looking at a dinosaur's skull. The shape of the space that was filled by the brain shows which parts of the brain were bigger.

# Super Senses

A titanosaur called *Sarmientosaurus musacchioi* seems to have had exceptionally good eyesight for a plant-eating dinosaur. It lived about 95 million years ago in Argentina. Its eye sockets were huge, almost half the length of its skull. This suggests that this dinosaur had better eyesight than most titanosaurs.

The remains of sauropods are often found without a skull. When the neck rotted away, the tiny head was often washed away by water or carried away by scavengers.

My friends call me Claws.

# Surprise!

When scientists looked at the remains of plant-eating dinosaurs called therizinosaurs, they were surprised by what they found. These creatures had well-developed senses of smelling and hearing, and also good balance, more like a meat eater. Therizinosaurs evolved from meat-eating ancestors, but they kept their meat eater senses even when they became plant eaters.

Therizinosaurs were covered with downy feathers and had enormous, razor-sharp claws 3 feet (1 m) long on their hands.

# Fascinating Fact

Some dinosaurs, perhaps all of them, had a ring of bones inside their eyes. The bones, called the sclerotic ring, helped to support the eye and hold it in the right shape.

## Did Dinosaurs Communicate?

Most scientists think dinosaurs communicated with each other like modern birds and reptiles. They probably had different calls to signal danger, attract a mate, and warn a rival creature to stay clear. Baby dinosaurs probably also had their own calls to ask for food or summon help.

# Sounding Off

Have you ever wondered what dinosaurs might have sounded like? Dinosaur mouths and throats were probably able to make all sorts of grunts, hisses, and roars, although we can't say for sure. Some scientists believe dinosaurs may have made cooing or hooting sounds like birds. Kritosaurus, one of the duck-billed hadrosaurs, had a flap of skin on its face that it could fill with air to make sounds. The biggest plant eaters may have been able to call to each other across great distances.

Honk if you're happy!

HONK!

We use our larynx, or voice box, to make sounds, but dinosaurs probably didn't have a larynx, so they would have had to make sounds in a different way.

## Fascinating Fact

There is no evidence that dinosaurs had ears like ours, but if they communicated they must have been able to hear. Scientists can tell from the shape of their brain that dinosaurs could indeed hear.

## Airhead

Some of the hadrosaurs had large hollow crests on top of their head. A hadrosaur could blow air through tubes inside the crest to make it vibrate like the hollow body of a guitar or violin. This would have made any sound produced by the dinosaur louder.

*Air flow*

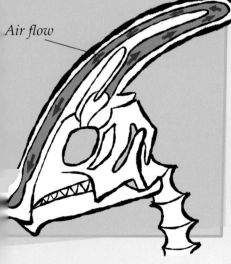

## Dinosaur Calls

Scientists scanned a Parasaurolophus skull and created a 3D model of it in a computer. Then the computer simulated the sound made by air blowing through it. It sounded like someone blowing a horn. It was the first time this dinosaur had been heard in 70 million years!

The roaring sounds made by dinosaurs in movies were created by mixing sounds made by elephants, crocodiles, tigers, and other animals.

The plates on a stegosaur's back were not attached to the creature's skeleton, but grew out of its skin. They were up to 2 feet (60 centimeters) wide and tall.

## Did Dinosaurs Look Like Reptiles?

Dinosaurs evolved from reptiles, so perhaps they looked like reptiles such as lizards and crocodiles, which are often brown or green. However, dinosaurs kept evolving and changing for more than 100 million years, so they may have ended up looking nothing like their reptile ancestors. No one knows for sure.

# Coloring In

The last of the dinosaurs died tens of millions of years before the first humans walked the earth, so no one knows what color any of the dinosaurs were. However, recent discoveries of microscopic structures in dinosaur skin that produce color have given scientists some clues about what colors the skin may have been. Some of the big plant-eating dinosaurs may even have been able to change their color. They did it by flooding some of their skin with blood to make it turn red.

# A Rush Of Blood

The bony plates on the back of a stegosaur had lots of blood vessels running through them. A stegosaur might have been able to flood these vessels with blood and turn the plates red. It may have done this to threaten other creatures or to attract mates.

*Red plates on back, Steggies attack!*

# Can You Believe It?

Usually, only the remains of dinosaur bones are found, because the creature's fleshy parts rotted away. However, a handful of dinosaurs have been preserved so perfectly that even their scaly skin can be seen.

Some dinosaurs, such as a plant eater called Ouranosaurus, had tall bony sails on their back that may have been brightly colored for signaling to other dinosaurs.

# Color Matching

A dinosaur's color came partly from tiny structures called melanosomes inside its skin cells. They contain melanin, which produces black and reddish-brown colors.

Scientists have actually found the remains of melanosomes in a 70 million-year-old hadrosaur, and they used these to show what the animal may have looked like.

27

## How Did Fossils Form?

Very few dinosaurs became fossils. When most dinosaurs died, they rotted or they were eaten, but some died in a place where they were covered quickly by earth or mud. Then water rich in minerals seeped into the bones and changed them into the stone fossils that we find today.

# Finding Fossils

No one has ever seen a real-life dinosaur, so how do we know what they looked like? They left behind all sorts of clues that can still be found buried in the ground today. These remains are called fossils. They show what a dinosaur's skeleton looked like, so we can tell how big it was, how its bones fitted together, and what shape it was. Dinosaur bones aren't the only things that were fossilized. Amazingly, dinosaur footprints have also been found. They show how dinosaurs walked and ran. Even fossilized dinosaur poop has been found!

# Fitting the Bones Together

Sometimes, scientists made mistakes when they rebuilt dinosaur skeletons. When the first fossils of a dinosaur called Iguanodon were found, scientists weren't sure where a spike-shaped bone belonged. They put it on the dinosaur's nose, like a horn. Later, they realized that it was actually the dinosaur's thumb bone!

The first dinosaur to be given a name based on its fossils was Megalosaurus, in 1824. It lived up to 180 million years ago in what is now Europe.

I'm so done with archeology.

## Fossilized Poop

The big plant-eating dinosaurs ate heaps of food and so of course they also produced lots of poop. Some of their poop was fossilized. Scientists call these fossils coprolites. It sounds better than poop, doesn't it? Studying coprolites shows what sort of plants the biggest dinosaurs were eating.

The oldest dinosaur fossil, found in Tanzania, is from a creature called Nyasasaurus parringtoni, which lived about 240 million years ago.

## Famous Fossil Finds

The first titanosaur fossils were found in 1828 in rocks called the Lameta Formation in Jabalpur, India, by Lieutenant Colonel W. H. Sleeman. They were lost for 134 years and only rediscovered in Kolkata in 2012.

# Glossary

**Bacteria**  Single-celled organisms found nearly everywhere on Earth. Bacteria take part in a wide variety of biological processes.

**Bipedal**  Walking on two legs.

**Bison**  A buffalo-like animal with a large head and humped shoulders.

**Carnivore**  A creature that eats mainly meat.

**Coprolite**  Fossilized animal droppings.

**Cretaceous**  A period of Earth's early history that began at the end of the Jurassic Period, 145 million years ago, and ended 65 million years ago. The dinosaurs disappeared at the end of the Cretaceous Period.

**Fossil**  Preserved remains of plants, animals, and other organisms that lived a long time ago.

**Gastrolith**  A stone swallowed by a dinosaur and some modern reptiles and birds to help them digest their food.

**Gut**  The part of an animal, mainly its stomach and intestines, that digests food.

**Hadrosaurs**  A group of creatures known as duck-billed dinosaurs because of the shape of their mouth.

**Herbivore**  A creature that eats mainly plants.

***Homo sapiens***  The species of humans that we belong to. *Homo sapiens*, the only surviving human species on Earth, means "wise man."

**Jurassic**  A period of Earth's early history that began at the end of the Triassic Period, about 201 million years ago, and ended 145 million years ago.

**Keratin**  Fibrous material that forms hair, fingernails, claws, reptile scales, and the outer covering of horns.

**Melanin**  A pigment (coloring material) that produces red, brown, and black colors in animal skin and hair.

**Melanosome** Part of an animal cell that produces and stores melanin.

**Neck frill** A broad plate of bone extending from the back of the head of some dinosaurs, such as Triceratops.

**Nutrient** A substance in food that a creature uses to survive and grow.

**Organism** A living bacterium, fungus, plant, or animal.

**Osteoderm** A bony lump, plate, scale, or spike in the skin of an animal.

**Predator** An animal that hunts, kills, and eats other animals.

**Prey** The animals that are hunted, killed, and eaten by a predator.

**Quadrupedal** Walking on four legs.

**Ravine** A narrow, steep-sided valley.

**Sauropod** A dinosaur belonging to a group of big plant-eating dinosaurs with a long neck, small head, and long tail. Sauropod means "lizard-footed."

**Scavenger** A creature that eats dead animals or plants.

**Species** A group of creatures that are similar to each other and can breed with each other.

**Stegosaurus** An armored plant-eating dinosaur with plates of bone standing upright along its back from head to tail.

**Titanosaur** A dinosaur belonging to a group of the biggest and heaviest dinosaurs that ever existed.

**Triassic** A period of Earth's early history that began about 252 million years ago and ended at the beginning of the Jurassic Period 201 million years ago. The dinosaurs appeared during the Triassic Period.

**Triceratops** A large, plant-eating dinosaur with three horns on its head and a broad neck frill.

# Index

**A**
Ampelosaurus 10
ankylosaur 10, 11, 13
Argentinosaurus 9
armor 10

**B**
balance 23
bipedal 7
birds 24
brain 20, 21, 22

**C**
Camarasaurus 19
carnivore 5
ceratopsian 16, 17
cold-blooded 9
color 26, 27
communication 24, 25
coprolite 29
crest 24, 25
Cretaceous Period 5, 17

**D**
digestion 6, 7

**E**
ears 25
Euoplocephalus 11
eyes 22, 23

**F**
feathers 23
fermentation 14

fighting 12, 13
food 14, 15
footprints 18, 19, 28
fossils 28

**G**
gastrolith 15

**H**
hadrosaur 15, 19, 24, 25, 27
herbivore 5
herds 18, 19
horns 16, 17

**I**
Iguanodon 18, 29
intelligence 20

**J**
Jurassic Period 4, 5, 17

**K**
Kritosaurus 24

**L**
legs 6

**M**
Megalosaurus 29
melanin 27
melanosome 27
Micropachycephalosaurus 11
migration 19
movies 25

**N**
neck frill 16, 17
Nyasasaurus 29

**O**
osteoderm 10
Ouranosaurus 27
Owen, Richard 10

**P**
Parasaurolophus 25
plants 14, 15
predators 7, 12, 13, 19

**R**
reptiles 6, 24

**S**
Sarmientosaurus 23
sauropod 8, 9, 13, 15, 23
sclerotic ring 23
senses 22, 23
skin 26, 27
sound 24, 25
Stegoceras 21
stegosaur 11, 13, 26, 27

**T**
teeth 6
temperature 11
therizinosaur 23
titanosaur 8, 23, 29
Triassic Period 4, 5
Triceratops 15, 16, 17